Facebook for Beginners: Navigating the Social Network

By

Shelby Johnson

Disclaimer: *No part of this ebook may be reproduced or transmitted in any form whatsoever, either electronic or mechanical, including photocopying, recording, or by any informational storage or retrieval system without the expressed written, dated and signed permission of the ebook author.*

The information presented herein represents the views and knowledge of the author as of the date of publication. This ebook is for informational purposes only and the author does not accept any responsibilities for any liabilities resulting from the use of this information. While every attempt has been made to verify the information provided here, the author cannot assume any responsibility for errors, inaccuracies or omissions. Due to the nature of the information in this book, it is possible that certain concepts or instruction sets will become outdated.

Table of Contents

Introduction

Even if you have never heard of the term "social networking" there is a pretty good chance you have heard of "Facebook" in one media outlet or another. Even those who have never been online to make a purchase or search for news have been captivated by its success, thanks to the daily and nightly news outlets' relentless coverage of its popularity.

People of all ages are using Facebook to connect with old friends, classmates and family members, while others enjoy keeping up with existing friends' day to day triumphs through status updates and image uploads.

All of this may seem foreign and intimidating to a new user, so this guide will help walk you through exactly what Facebook is, what it is used for, and how to use it, so you don't feel overwhelmed by creating and maintaining an account!

Having a Facebook account can keep you connected with friends and family members anywhere in the world, while allowing you to express yourself freely over the most popular social network available! With over one billion people using Facebook, you are bound to connect with friends from childhood, high school, college and even those who enjoy similar activities as you.

This social networking site is currently the King (or queen) of socializing online, and with each new development unveiled by the Facebook brass, the experience richens. No matter what you use the social networking for, whether it is to promote your ideas and concepts, or to socialize with friends and family, the long arm of the brand is far-reaching and serves as a trustworthy source for searches and information that is available to the masses. When you are ready to use the site, here is how to make it work for and with you.

What is Facebook, and Why Join?

Facebook is a publicly-traded social networking site that counts over 900 million active users as registrants. Social networking is an online service that allows users to interact with people they know, and even those they don't through shared interests, hobbies, topics and backgrounds without the luxury of living in the same geographical area. For instance, if you enjoy arts and crafts, you can connect with a number of individuals who share the same passion even if you live in the United States and they live in China!

Facebook is free, and can be used by anyone with an internet connection, but they must register for the service first, and create an account before the networking can begin. This service allows you, the user, to interact with others online through status updates, instant messages, standard messages and group messages.

There are innumerable reasons to join Facebook, each of which can be classified differently depending on your current commitment.

- Keep in touch with children & grandchildren.
- Fortify long distance relationships with friends & family.
- Find old friends, relatives or classmates.
- Socialize with friends who have already joined.
- Share your world with those you love.
- Meet new people no matter their geographical location.
- Monitor younger users as an online safety precaution.

- Enjoy shared interests with other online users.
- Just because you want to know what it's all about!

It is important to know that you can deactivate your account at any time, so if you feel Facebook isn't right for you, you can cease using the site altogether.

How to Sign Up & Create a Profile

Now that you are ready to jump into the exciting world of social networking, all you have to do is sign up and create a profile. It's easy to do, and should be a captivating experience, instead of one that leads to confusion and frustration. Let's begin!

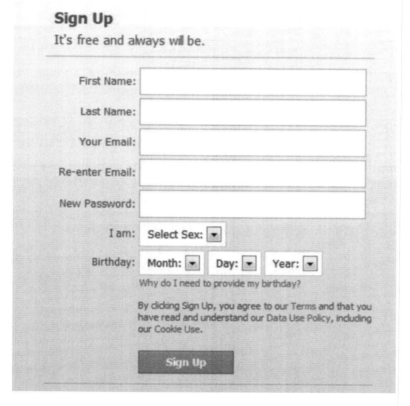

1. Type Facebook.com into your web browser's URL bar.
2. Locate the "Sign Up" section (which is easily viewable on the homepage, seen above).

3. Enter your First Name, Last Name, Email Address, and Create a Password.
   - If you do not have an email address already, you must create one through any online email site. There are a number of free options including Gmail, Yahoo! and AOL.
   - A password can consist of any letters or numbers, but will need to be re-entered each time you logon to the site, so create a password you will remember, or write it down in a safe place.
4. Enter your sex by placing your cursor over the drop down box and selecting "Male" or "Female."
5. Enter your birthday using the same cursor over the drop down box procedure.
   - Facebook requires users to list their birthday, so the information that is targeted towards you is age-appropriate. You will be able to hide this information so it is not visible to others.
6. Click "Sign Up."

You will be taken to a page that will give you the option to automatically search your email contacts for others who are already using Facebook. If you choose to use this step, simply click "Find Friends" as it is highlighted under your email account address, and the search will begin. Or, you can simply skip this step by clicking "Skip This Step" at the bottom of the page. You will have plenty of opportunities to locate friends once your profile is up and running, so skipping the search initially will not harm your social outcome later.

Begin filling out your profile information as it is requested. You will be prompted to enter your academic information, such as where you went to high school or college. If you are searching for old schoolmates, this segment of the profile is important. Enter the schools and click "Save and Continue." If you choose not to list the information simply click the "Skip" link.

Adding Your Profile Picture

Next you will be asked to upload a photo that will be labeled as your "Profile Picture." This image is what everyone else will see when they view your profile, or when you are interacting through chats, messages or commenting practices.

This does not have to be a picture of you, if you are uncomfortable with displaying your physical identity. You can choose from any number of representations including your favorite cartoon character, or a scenic shot from one of your travels, as long as you have the image saved to your computer electronically and the rights to use it. You do not have to upload a profile picture at all, but it certainly helps others identify your involvement in groups or interests. This picture can be changed at any time, so as your familiarity with the program increases, you can swap it out for another if you would like.

Uploading an Existing Picture

- Click the "Upload a Photo" link.
- Click "Choose a Photo" from the window provided.
- Locate and double click the folder on your computer where the image is stored.
- Locate and click the image you desire to upload.

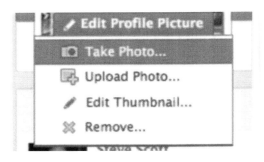

It could take a few minutes for the image to upload, so simply wait for the process to finish.

Taking & Uploading a Picture from Your Webcam

The other option listed is to take a picture of yourself with your webcam, if your computer is equipped with such a device.

This feature will process the webcam software, and supply you with a reflection of yourself on screen. Take and save the picture with the easy to use instructions, and it will appear as your profile picture. You will be able to see it before you move forward, so don't worry that it will upload to your account immediately.

After you see the image has uploaded, click "Save and Continue." If you choose not to upload an image, click "Skip."

Your profile will now be active, and you can begin using it to find friends or for them to find you!

Using Your Profile

You are now ready to start using Facebook! First, let's go over the terminology that is associated with the site, so you know exactly what is going on, and are comfortable with listing information about yourself, or while communicating with others. At any time, you can return to your personal profile simply by clicking on your profile picture. When you are away from your profile, which is considered your home page, you will either be on a "Friend's" page or what is called the "Newsfeed."

What are Facebook Friends?

Friends are people you know on Facebook, and are referred to as such whether you have known them your entire life, or literally just met them through a shared interest forum. There's more about how you can find and add friends later on in this book.

What is Status?

A status is a post you enter on your profile so others can see it in their Newsfeed. If you would like to tell everyone you know that you are at the zoo, you can sign into Facebook and enter "Lovely day at the zoo!" and everyone else will see it when they sign into their account through their Newsfeed.

What is the Newsfeed?

The Facebook Newsfeed is a forum where everyone you are friends with can see your updated status, and you can see theirs. For instance, if you have twenty Facebook friends and each of them have updated their status recently, they will appear in the order in which they were updated for you to view. This is a great way to see what everyone is up to!

Profile Components

When you return to your profile page by clicking your profile image you will be given a number of options to list your employment or contact information if you would like for others to know more about you. Likewise, you can list interests of all kinds including music, books, products, services, movies and television shows that appeal to you.

On the left hand side of your Facebook page, below your profile picture you will see the option "Wall" just above the "Info" option. You can return to the "Info" option at any time to make changes to your interests or listed information.

How to Update Your Status

On both your profile page and your newsfeed/home page for Facebook should be a section towards the top labeled as "Update Status" with a space for text that says, "What's on your mind?" Begin typing exactly that, and hit "Post." Your status has been updated, and others will see it in the Newsfeed!

In the graphic illustration shown, notice the lower left hand area of the status update box. You'll see several small icons there which you can click on. One is a person's silhouette with a "+" sign. Clicking on that will allow you to type in the names of people you are with (or who you want to mention) in your status. Adding someone's name to a status update will help the person get a notification about it too, so they know you have done an update they should see.

The next icon is a small placement pin. By clicking on that, you can type in the location of your status (for example if you were at a specific city, town or venue).

Next to the placement pin icon is a small camera icon. Click on this to include a photo or other file to share with your status update.

Finally, you should see a smiley face icon. Click on this icon to bring up "what you are doing." This will give a range of options you can include in your status update including "listening to" certain music, watching a certain show, or feeling a certain emotion. This isn't something you necessarily have to include on your status updates, but many people do.

As seen on the graphic illustration above, there is also a spot which says "Public" on the lower right area of your status update box. You can click on that area to decide exactly who you want to see your status update, whether it's everyone (Public), only Friends, only yourself or Custom. With "Custom" you can define specific people who will be the only ones to see the status update! Basically, you control who sees the status messages you post.

Individuals list a number of items as status updates, which can range from where they are having lunch, to what kind of day they are having. You are the only one who can decide how much or how little information you share through your status updates. If you have something to say at any point throughout the day, night or week, type it in and hit "Post." It will be viewable by your friends, who can then comment on your status, which is where the interaction begins.

Below is an example of a status update:

> You: *I'm finally on Facebook!*

> Friend: *How exciting! You're going to love it!*

> Another Friend: *It's about time!*

You can comment on these comments, and keep the conversation going for as long or as little as you would like. Keep in mind you can comment at any time, whether it's within a few seconds of another person's comment, or hours, days or weeks later.

(Note: Status updates on your profile page may include other options. For example, talking about a certain location you went to, or adding a major "Life Event" such as a wedding or birth of a child to your timeline.)

Adding Images, Videos and Links to Your Status Update

Directly next to the "Update Status" icon is an "Add Photo/Video" link. Click the link and a bevy of options will appear.

Upload Photo/Video

This option will allow you to upload a photo or video that you would like to share with others. This can be something you found online or an image or video you took or recorded on your own. You can share information that is serious, funny, political or religious. It's up to you completely. Just keep in mind that others have the same freedom, and you are not always going to agree with every topic, image or link you see.

Use Webcam

This option will allow you to take a picture with your computer, so you can share whatever is in front of it at the time. It will upload the same way another electronic image would.

Create Photo Album

This feature is perfect for people who have just returned from vacation and want to share their travels with their friends. It will allow you to upload multiple pictures into a group, and label them according by date, place or event. Example labels such as "Class Reunion 2012" or "Arizona Vacation" are common representations of events or trips that help people view your images as albums, just as they would if they were printed.

While uploading images, whether in a photo album or as a single shot, you will be prompted to add a credit line to the image, which you can add or skip. Next, you will be asked who is in the photo with you. This is a unique feature that allows you to list the people in the image, which is called "tagging." When you "tag" someone, the post will also appear on their profile page, so their friends can see it too. Friends can tag you as well, which makes the experience interactive and fun for everyone involved. You will also be given the option to list where the photo was taken. None of these options are mandatory, so if you choose to upload an image without any information, you are free to do so.

Finally, you can decide who can or cannot see the image by selecting the privacy setting that is associated with the images. This list includes friends, friends of friends, family, or only you.

Finally, click "Post" and the status update, image, video or album will post to your profile, and will be visible to others through the Newsfeed.

How to Add or Change Your Cover Photo

A cover photo is a sort of banner that sits at the top of your Facebook profile and shows the image of your choice. It can be a photo you took of a pet, a place, or event, or group of people, or any other photo that you might want to display as a backdrop banner at the top of your profile

To add or change your cover photo:

1. Go to your Facebook profile.
2. Hover your mouse cursor over the space to the right of your profile photo up top. You should see "Change Cover" button pop up.
3. Click the "Change Cover" button.
4. You'll now have the option to "Upload Photo." Click on this, and choose a photo from those you have stored on your computer.

Note: *Keep in mind that cover photos work best with certain size images, so the image may stretch out or look strange due to the sizing.*

It's also important to note that you can do a Google search for "Facebook cover photo" and there are pre-made photos you can save or download onto your computer and then use as your cover photo. So there's plenty of options, but it's best to make sure that you aren't using copyrighted work, or uploading something wildly inappropriate. Other Facebook users could report a cover photo for that.

How to Find People on Facebook

Now that you have your profile set up, it is time to start showing it off to others! There are a number of ways to locate friends, family members, co-workers and associates through Facebook, including by name, location, email or identifying labels such as education and workplace listings.

Searching by Name

If you are looking for a specific person, or multiple people, who you already know have Facebook pages, simply locate the search bar at the top of the page. It will say "Search for People, Places and Things." Enter the names of the people you are searching for individually. You should see any matches for the name you type display as you type. You can then click on any of those listed if they appear to be the person you know.

Alternatively, click on the "Find all people named 'person's name'" option and you'll be taken to a page where you see more listings of people with that name, as well as a righthand sidebar area where you can "Refine This Search." In that righthand side area you'll be able to select such details as the person's gender, age range, relationship status and more, to help you narrow your search down.

When you locate a person you want to add as a friend you will click on their profile and be given the option to request their friendship. Make the request, and the person will be notified by email. It will be up to that person to sign into Facebook and accept your request. When someone requests your friendship you will receive the same email or notification on your upper right hand menu area of Facebook. You can also decline requests, so it certainly isn't necessary to allow people you don't know to become your online friends if you are not comfortable with doing so.

Searching by Location

You can list the city you are looking for friends in, but be ready for a large return of results. With over 900 million active users, it is almost certain that there are a number of users with names similar to your friends or colleagues, so names are a great way to start the process, instead of relying on locations to return anything but excessive results.

Searching by Education/Workplace/Organizations

This process is the same, but will only net the results of those who have entered their affiliations with these places in their profiles. Also, if you type in "Red Cross" you will almost certainly receive the organization's Facebook page as a result.

Searching by Email Address Contacts

If you skipped this step in the beginning, you can still locate individual friends by their email address. To add friends who are email contacts, go up to the small friends icon (silhouette of two people) on the menu at the top right hand corner of the Facebook page. Click on that icon and then choose "Find Friends." You'll be taken to a page which displays any pending friend requests that have been sent to you. Also, on the right side of this page you will see an area to type in the email addresses you use to find contacts who are on Facebook.

Another way to do this on an individual basis is to type a person's email address into the search bar at the top of any page, and if the person is using Facebook under that email address, you should see them appear. Click on that person to go to their profile page and then click the "Add Friend" button.

Searching for Classmates

One of the easiest ways to do this is by using the top search bar and typing in your high school or college name. The search graph will attempt to figure out what you are looking for and give you various options to help locate people you went to school with. You may also see any relevant groups or pages that were started about the school(s) you enter.

One example for what to type into the search bar is "People who went to (school name) in 1989." This will bring up a listing of all the people on Facebook who have on their profile that they attended the school during that particular year. It's a good way to find long last classmates from your school who you may want to reconnect with!

Now that you've found friends, family members and colleagues, it is time to start interacting with them! But before you do, there are a few more terms that you should familiarize yourself with, to make the interaction seamless and fun.

What Do Like, Comment and Share Mean?

When you or someone you are friends with posts their status, there will be a number of options that exist to viewers: Like, Comment and Share. Here's the breakdown of what each of these refers to.

Like

The "Like" link is there for individuals to simply click that states "I see your post, and I like the contents of it" without having to say a word. When they like it, their name with appear with others who have done the same, while identifying exactly how many people have liked it. For example, if three people have clicked the "Like" button, the post will list "3 People Like This Post." You can also "Like" individual comments within the post as well.

Comment

When you have a little more to give than a silent thumbs up, click the comment link and begin typing exactly what you think about the post. For example, if the initial comment was "Lovely day for a trip to the zoo!" Someone could post, "Be sure to see the elephant exhibit while you're there!"

Share

The "Share" link will only make itself available if there is an image, video or link that can be transferred to your profile. This means that if someone posts an image you really like, you can click the share link, and it will allow you to upload it as your status update, complete with your comments on the item.

Top Menu Bar and Navigation

Whether you are on your profile page, in the Newsfeed section or on another's profile, the top menu bar will remain the same at all times. This started to appear in the right-hand corner of your webpage after the 2013 updates.

In that top menu bar, which is simply the information that appears at the top of the screen, you will have different icons, which may become illuminated in light blue with numbers on them. They will appear in the following order (left to right):

Friend Requests

The first icon is a silhouette of two people, and is where your friend request notifications will be.

When someone requests your friendship, this area will be illuminated with a number that denotes how many requests you have. Simply click on the icon to open this segment and accept or decline friends as you see fit.

Messages

This section works almost exactly like email. You can send personal messages to other Facebook users, and your communications will be privately transferred within this section.

When someone sends you a message, it will be highlighted up top (see the caption bubbles above), with a specific number showing in the upper left-hand area of your screen. Click the icon to view these messages. Once you are reading a message, a space will automatically be provided for you to reply. Enter the information and hit the "Reply" button and your message will be sent.

At the bottom of your message list there will be a link that says, "See All Messages." This will allow you to archive the messages as you see fit, or to mark them as unread, so you can go back to them later.

You must have a specific message open before you can complete the following actions:

- Forward: Allows you to send the communication to someone else.
- Delete: Allows to you trash the conversation completely.
- Report as Spam: Allows you to report the communication as something you do not want to receive.

- Report the Conversation: Allows you to report any harassing contact to the programmers.

Any of these can be easily accomplished by clicking the "Actions" icon and choosing your preference for that particular message from the list.

Notifications

The third icon is for "Notifications." This is the globe icon (see above) which will appear illuminated with a number when someone. . .

- Writes on your wall.

- Comments on your status update.

- Clicks "Like" on your status update.

- Clicks "Like" on a comment you've made.

- Tags you in a photo or in a comment.

- Lists you at a venue with them.

Up top you will also see a search window, which will always be in the same place, so if at any time you remember something you wanted to look up, just type it in!

Next we'll cover the basics of the top menu choices on your Facebook seen in the image below. They usually appear to the right of the notifications, at the upper right corner of your Facebook.

Home

The home icon will always return you to the Newsfeed, just as the small Facebook logo will next to the search bar. Sometimes you may see a number displayed here to indicate something new has arrived on the newsfeed.

Find Friends

This text will allow you at any point to apply information that may net you search results of people you know. Also, it will automatically list some people that are friends with people you are friends with that you may want to consider sending a request to. You don't have to, as they are simply suggestions.

Your Name & Profile Image

There will be a small listing of your name and profile image which can be clicked on at any time to return you directly to your profile. You should see your first name at the upper right hand corner of the screen as well, right next to a small lock and gear icon. Wherever you see your profile image, whether it is in a comment or along the side of the page, you can click on it to return to your profile.

Small Lock (Privacy Options)

There is a small lock icon next to your name in the right hand corner for quick shortcuts to various privacy settings for your profile. This is an important part of your account, allowing you to set "Who can see my stuff?" or who can contact you. Also, you can get help if someone is bothering you on Facebook, along with more settings in this convenient area.

Down Arrow or Gear (Settings)

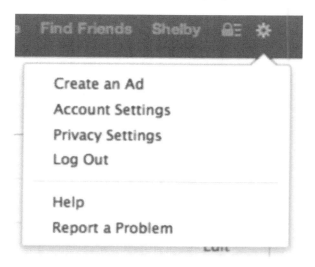

The down arrow or gear icon on the upper, right-hand corner of your Facebook page contains several helpful links, including account and privacy settings. This is an important part of your account, and determines who can see your information.

Advertise (or Create an Ad)

The first option under the area is "Advertise" or "Create an Ad." This allows you to reach out to other Facebook users in specialized areas in an effort to boost your business. This feature is not free. You can explore its content for free, and cannot in any way sign up without knowing it, so don't let it scare you. You will not automatically be enrolled in advertising at any time. There's more on this segment in an upcoming section.

Account Settings

This section will provide you with your behind the scenes Facebook profile, including which email address you have assigned to the account. Within this area you will find your security options, which you can set to meet your personal comfort including secure browsing and login notification features.

Notification History

Also under this section is your notification history, which will tell you exactly who has notified you and in what capacity, either via private messages or through posts. You can edit your preferences within each category as you see fit.

Subscribers, Apps, Mobile, Payments and Facebook Ads

The remaining options in the account settings category are opt-in segments, which do not apply to everyone. They are certainly worth a few minutes of your time, so you are aware of their existence and can use any of them at any time, including games with other Facebook friends, or operating Facebook on your mobile device.

Privacy Settings

The third category under the down arrow is your privacy settings. This function allows you to determine who can see your posts, including public visitors, which is just about anyone who clicks on your profile, to just friends. It also allows you to customize your viewing.

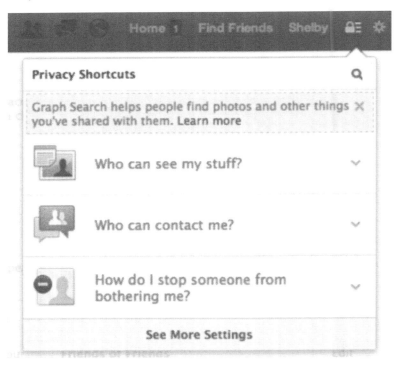

This area also allows you to determine how you connect with others, including whether or not you want others to have the ability to tag you in photos or in comments. Finally, you can use this area to block people or apps from your Facebook page completely. This option comes in handy for many people, especially if they feel like they have received one too many game requests from friends.

Log Out

The fourth option under the down arrow is "Log Out." You should always log out of your Facebook account at the end of each session, especially if you are on a shared or public computer. If you do not log out, anyone else can open the Facebook site and view your information, or comment on your behalf. Logging out restricts anyone from using your account maliciously.

Help

The final category under the down arrow is "Help." This link will navigate you to frequently asked questions and answers regarding certain portions of Facebook, so if you are having a problem with the site you can find an answer quickly and effectively.

Communicating on Facebook

You have a profile, you have uploaded images and you have friends to broadcast your happenings to, so now it's time to start communicating with the masses! There are a number of tools at your disposal, and within a few sessions you will be able to figure out what works best for you when you communicate.

Timeline

Your timeline, which appears on your profile page, will list all of your status updates in the order they were applied. This page is designed to supply you with a neat and tidy summation of everything you have done – or at least listed on Facebook, including the people you have become friends with, and comments you have made on other people's status updates – in the order in which they occurred.

This is the area others will visit to see what has been going on with you since the last time you talked. This section is not always private. Even if you do not allow others to post on your timeline, friends are still able to view it. You can keep scrolling down on Facebook to see more and more of the timeline on your page.

Filtering Content on Timeline Feed

Just as you can with your email, or pop-ups, you can filter the content that appears on your Facebook Timeline Newsfeed with a few easy movements.

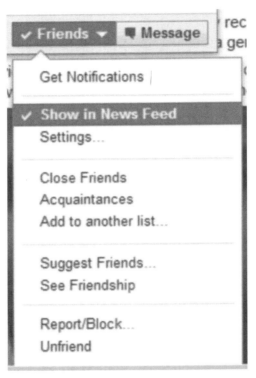

This is particularly handy for when a certain family member is rambling on and on about an upcoming election, or a friend from school insists on lamenting their most recent break-up for the world to see. All you have to do is hide their updates from your newsfeed, until you feel comfortable adding them back into the mix -- if ever. Here's how:

- Hover over the person's profile picture image to the left of the post on your newsfeed and a box will pop up showing the person's profile.
- You'll see the "Friends" button with a check mark next to it.
- Hover over that button to bring up more options, including one that will say "Show in News Feed." If it's checked, click on the option again to uncheck it. You will receive additional options to control what shows up from this person on your Facebook newsfeed.

Another way to filter content from a friend on your newsfeed is:

- Click the down arrow to the right of their Profile Picture/Name on a newsfeed item they posted.
- Click on "Hide" to hide their story from your newsfeed.
- You will then receive other options including "Hide all stories from" that person or page.
- Select the options you want to hide, or "unlike" or "unfollow" that person or page if necessary.

You did not have to "unfriend" them, which can be awkward when it is a family member or relative of a close friend, or remark on their absurdity to yourself or others going forward. Now you simply cannot see what they are saying! It is a near perfect solution!

If the problem is not your friends, but your subscriptions, pages, groups or apps that are clogging up your timeline with useless (to you, anyway) information, get ready to unsubscribe from their roll call with just a few clicks. For these various settings and instructions, you'll want to use the top search bar, your main newsfeed/home area's lefthand side column, or the small "gear" icon at the top of your screen (in the upper righthand corner).

- For Pages: The easiest way is to go up to your search bar, type in the name of the page and go to that page. Once you are at the page, you can hover over the button that says "Liked." You'll see a menu show up that gives you options to "Show in Newsfeed" which may already be checked. You can click "Show in Newsfeed" to uncheck it and prevent the page's latest posts from showing on your newsfeed. Alternatively, if you don't want to be associated with the page anymore you can choose "Unlike the page" from that menu you see when you hover over the "Liked" button.
- For Groups: Go to your main Facebook newsfeed/home area. Hover next to the group name on your left sidebar area to reveal the small "pencil" icon. Click the pencil and then you can click on the "Edit settings" to adjust the notifications you receive from the group. Or you can click on the option to Leave Group.
  (Additionally, you can go directly to the group page from the sidebar on your newsfeed. Remove Yourself from the Group by Clicking on its Name on your sidebar. On the group page go to the small "gear" icon towards the upper right top of the page, and Click "Leave Group.")

- For Apps: The easiest way to alter your app settings or remove an app is to click on the small "gear" icon you see up near the top upper right corner of your Facebook page. On that menu, choose "Account Settings." You'll go to a settings page, where you should see a list of options on the lefthand side. Choose "Apps" to see your App settings. Locate the One you Want to Remove, and hit the "X" in the Upper Right-hand Corner.
  (You can also click "Edit" next to any app to edit your app privacy settings, including whether or not your Facebook friends can see your latest notifications from an app or game.)

You can always re-like something later, if you start to miss seeing their information on your newsfeed. This happens quite a bit. You never know how informative something is until you do not have it any longer! If it does happen, search for it in the toolbar, and like it all over again. Be sure "Show in Newsfeed" is checked too, otherwise it will not appear on your timeline, but only in your "likes" queue.

Messages

In the messaging section, you can send private messages that are only for the recipients eyes. Or, you can send a message to a group of people, knowing that all responses will be available to everyone listed as a recipient. The latter is great for setting up group activities or party planning.

Creating a Post

When you create a post, you are telling your Facebook friends what you are doing, where are doing it, or even exactly how you are doing it with an image! This fun way to keep people apprised of your happenings is a great way to share information and occurrences. It is also a great way to share informative news, instructions, or simply something you thought was funny. The frequency at which you update your status, or post to Facebook, is completely up to you. Some people have lots to say to their social networking friends, and therefore update often, and others rather enjoy reading the updates, but not necessarily providing them. One is not better than the other, it is simply a person preference.

When you are logged on to Facebook, whether you are on the newsfeed page, or your profile page, there will be a status box that appears at the top. It will say something like, "What are you up to?" or "How is your day going?" The message changes, and is a fun tidbit of Facebook. To update your status, simply type in whatever it is you are doing or thinking and hit return. When you want to do more than add a quick statement, and would like to include the people you are with, your location or even an image, you can do that too!

To "tag" people in your updated post, to indicate that they are either with you, or directly related to the content you are posting, simply click on the icon that resembles a silhouette of a person's head and shoulders, and a + sign. This entry box will allow you to add people from your friends list, simply by beginning to enter their name. For instance, if you want to tag a friend named "Sarah" simply begin typing in her name, S-a-r-a-h until her profile appears. When you hit the "S", each friend you have that begins with that letter will appear, and begin to dwindle as you add more letters, until you actually get to only Sarah on the list. Click on her name and profile when it does appear, and any other people you want to add along the way, to include them in your post.

If you would like to add your location, simply click on the pin drop icon, third in the lineup of options from adding friends to the post (only the clock lies in between the tagging and location options). This will give your current location -- based on your GPS coordinates -- or allow you to choose from the nearest businesses, such as restaurants or shopping malls. Once you have found the venue you are in, or enjoying, you can tap the selection to add it to your post.

To include an image in your post, tap or click the "Photo" icon above the message and choose whether to upload a photo or video, or create an entire album. You will then need to tell your device where the picture is located on its drive, so it uploads the correct one.

To upload a video, follow the same procedure, and choose the video media instead of an image. If you would like to upload a photo album, you can add an unlimited amount of pictures before actually posting the status update.

This process is great for vacation, wedding or party photos, so they remain tied to each other in an album. If you are taking a picture for the expressed use of sharing it on Facebook, hit the "Take a Photo" option when you tap the photo/camera icon and shoot! It will automatically upload it for your review before you actually post the status update to the site.

Finally, there is an opened mouth smiley face -- the fourth option in the lineup, which allows you to "Say what you are doing". This function delivers a number of options of feeling (happy, sad, enthusiastic, etc.), eating, drinking, shopping, listening to, and so on. It will add an expressive emoticon to your status update to give depth to your post. This is a pretty new option that arrived with the last update, and users love the idea of adding one more sentiment to their posts for others to see and understand.

In the end, if you have chosen to add each one of these to your post, it will look like this:

"Buying this dress for tonight's party (picture of dress) -- with Sarah Sarah at the Glenpark Mall. (Party emoticon inserted) Feeling Excited!"

OR

"Eating the best cheeseburger on the planet (picture of cheeseburger) -- with Sarah Sarah at Fat Burger. (Smiley emoticon inserted) Feeling Satisfied.

You can add a status update with simply words, no photos or videos or emoticons if you prefer. In fact, you never have to add your location if you do not want anyone to know where you are at any time. The personalization factors that comprise the Facebook experience is what makes it so popular.

Finally, and this is important to a lot of people, you can use the drop down box that says, by default, "Public" with a global icon, to customize who sees your posts. Public means anyone can see it. If you choose Friends, only your friends will be able to see it, family, friends or groups you are a member of are all on the list, and you can choose accordingly who sees your post. Again, this is completely up to you.

Chatting & Video Chatting

In the bottom, right-hand corner there is a section that says "Chat" with a number beside it in parenthesis "(#)." If you click on the icon it will reveal everyone who is online at the moment. If you click on their name you will open a window that allows you to start chatting with this person immediately. Only one window in chat will open, so you cannot chat with more than one person in the same window. Separate windows will apply to each person.

When the chat window is open, there will be a video camera icon at the top. Click the icon to start a video chat with the person you have selected. This is only possible if you both have a webcam. This will allow you chat face to face with the use of your cameras.

All chat windows can be closed by clicking the "X" at the top of the chat session.

Advanced Facebook Options

Now that you have gotten the hang of using Facebook, you can start exploring its advanced features which include Fan Pages, Groups and Advertising.

Fan Pages

The creators of Facebook know that we all like certain things in this world, and not just the comments our friends are making, so they have allowed the creation of "Fan Pages" to help customers, visitors and interested parties stay abreast of the topics that appeal to them.

For instance, if you are an animal rights activist, you may list an interest page on your timeline that will appear as "Your name here "Likes" People for the Betterment of Zoo Conditions." The organization that appears in the post or the page that you like is considered a Fan Page. These exist for everything from foods and beverages to causes and complaints.

You can also subscribe to your favorite sports teams, stores and brands' pages, to get updates on players, sales and products.

Keep in mind, the items that you like or subscribe to will present a menagerie of similar interests for you to join through advertising. You don't have to click on any advertisement that is presented to you, but it is important for you to know that your interests, likes and subscriptions are noted by the programmers, so you are provided with the opportunity to enjoy similar interests from third parties.

How to Create a Fan Page

What is even more exciting is that you can create your very own Fan Page by following a few quick steps. This is a great tool for bands, causes, companies and organizations alike.

On your lefthand sidebar area, look for the "Pages" section. Click the "Create a Page" option. It is completely free, and a great way to reach out to prospective online friends and followers.

You will be given six categories to choose from:

- Local Business or Place
- Company, Organization or Institution
- Brand or Product
- Artist, Band or Public Figure
- Entertainment
- Cause or Community

Once you have chosen your preference, options will begin appearing to help you identify the proper process for proceeding with your Fan Page. Once you have it up and running, display a link on your personal Facebook page to send traffic to your new creation! This is perfect for keeping your fans up to date on your band's booked dates and venues, or your company's new products.

Groups

Groups are slightly different from Fan Pages, as they typically involve only those who are interested in a specific topic. For instance, if you wanted to create the Group "Ex (Insert Company Name Here) Employees Who Want to Stay in Touch" you would simply have to create the Group using the following steps while you are in the Newsfeed forum.

- Locate the word "Groups" on the left-hand side of the page.
- Click "Create Group."
- Enter the Group Name: Ex (Insert Company Name Here) Employees to Stay in Touch.
- For Members, enter the individual names of the people you want to invite. As you type a person's Facebook name, you should see that person's name show up if they're already your friend on Facebook.
- Set the privacy setting as you see fit.

Individuals will automatically be sent a request to join the group, and once they do you can all socialize in that forum, which depending on your privacy settings, could mean only the select amount of you can see the information that is being communicated. It's a lot of fun, and helps shrink your communications into a specialized group of people.

"Like" Fan/Community Pages

Just as you become friends with people you know and meet on Facebook, Fan/Community Pages offer a similar feel when you "Like" them. Individuals, groups, restaurants and even brands create these pages for you to like, so they can keep in touch with you about their products or services. Their involvement is two-fold in that they are getting you to spread the word of their organizational happenings, and that their existence on Facebook gives them more visibility online, and provides a trusted link for the search engines to return. In short, if you search for something through your favorite search engine, and their Facebook page is one of the results, chances are you will click on it. You know it is not spam, and you know it will provide you with accurate information. It is a win/win for you, and marketers alike.

When you "Like" the page, their information and status updates will appear on your Newsfeed, or Timeline when you check "Show on Newsfeed" in the "Like" dropdown box. This is perfect for keeping tabs on your favorite restaurants, so you can see their specials appear on your timeline each day, or your favorite brands so you know when there is a sale. Also, bands create fan pages so you can keep tabs on where they are playing, or when a new release is out. Every entity possible has a Facebook fan page, including television shows, sports teams, and even small boutiques around the world. They are informative and exciting, and the only stipulation is that the limit of Fan pages that you can like is 5,000. That may seem like a lot now, but when you start liking everything from candy to footwear, your count will start adding up quickly. You can always remove your fandom if you get to the limit, to make room for something else, by unliking it through their page.

You may receive requests from friends to "Like" a page they have liked, which is as simple as liking it or ignoring the request. You do not have to like everything, but keep in mind that if your friends own businesses, they will probably ask you more than once to like their page to improve their online visibility. Again -- liking anything is completely up to you.

Linking Other Social Media Accounts & Facebook

More and more, as you begin to grow comfortable with social media, you will want to share what's happening on one site, like Pinterest, Instagram or Twitter, on your Facebook account. It is only natural that everything comes back to Facebook, since it has the most users by far. It is easy to use, and easy to connect with from other sites too.

There are ways to manually connect your other social networks to Facebook, so your information spreads as you add it everywhere. Here's how:

Twitter

- Logon to your Twitter Account.
- Select Settings.
- Select Profile.
- Scroll Down to the Bottom of your Profile Page.
- Select Connect to Facebook.

You will be asked to provide your Facebook login information at that time.

Instagram

- Logon to your Instagram Account.
- Select Profile.

- Select your Device Type (Android or iPhone).
- Select Shared Settings.
- Select Facebook.

Once you confirm your Facebook information, you will be given the option to upload to the site each time you take a picture.

Pinterest

- Logon to your Pinterest Account.
- Select Settings.
- Select Turn on Facebook Login Link.
- Move the Slider to "Yes" Where "Post Your Activity to Your Timeline."
- Save Changes.

Now everything you do will appear on you Facebook page, and allow you to keep up with all of your social media in one place! If you are more of a mobile person, and prefer an app to do all of this socializing for you, there are a number you can download that will allow you to speak to the masses for you.

Helpful Social Media Apps

Consider these social media apps, and find the one that's right for you:

- Buffer App
- Google+
- LiveGO
- Netvibes

- UberSocial

When you want to put all of your social networks on your mobile phone, so you can manage them separately, simply download the individual apps to your mobile device, and login to them using your usernames and passwords, and check them as you see fit by tapping on the icon.

Playing Games/Using Apps on Facebook

Facebook is for more than socializing, it also has games and apps that are fun to play and enjoy in your spare time. You can go from your timeline and see what's happening in the world before moving directly into a break from the whirling events of the day into game time.

To get there:

Log in to your Facebook Account.

- Locate the Apps Icon on the Left-hand Side of your Newsfeed Screen.
- Click Apps Center.

Once inside, you have the option to click on "All Games" from the toolbar on the left, if you are looking for something specific. Either way, the options will appear in categories of:

- Top Games.
- Friends' Games.
- Suggested.
- Top Rated.
- Trending.
- Top Grossing.

You can also choose from the type of game, whether its Words, Puzzles, Action, Cards, Casino, Hidden Objects or just about anything in between.

Keep in mind, however, that you can play almost all of these games for free. The issue becomes, later -- as proven by the "Top Grossing" list -- that you may have to purchase additional lives, keys to unlock certain areas of the game. Be careful with spending on these games, as .99 may not seem like a lot now -- but if you hit it twenty times, well -- that's $20.

If you do prefer apps to games online, look for the free ones if you do not mind advertisements. If you are opposed to ads popping up during your game time, you can purchase the app at the time of downloading, or upgrade to the paid version later. Pricing can vary from .99 to $1.99 and up to as much as the programmer believes it is worth.

Apps also do more than give you the ability to play games. The can add to your working experience, photographical prowess, and even enlighten your free time with stories. Search for the things you like in the search bar, and determine once you find it whether it is worth the price listed -- or you can find a similar version that is free. There are literally close to 1.5 million apps available, so something is bound to grab your taste or desires.

You can play games directly on Facebook, without downloading any software to your computer, which is nice and leaves space open on your hard drive for other important items. However, if you want to download the app to your mobile device, all you have to do is go to your App Store for Apple devices, or Google Play for Android devices, and search for the app you have in mind through the search bar.

If you do not know what you are looking for, peruse the available options based on their popularity, price or how long they have been on the market. Tap the app you have in mind, and read the details, ratings and reviews before purchasing. Once you have decided, click the price (even where it says free) to signify your choose, you will then need to hit it again to install it fully. Once it is installed, you can play to your heart's content -- or until your battery goes dead.

Facebook Ads

Advertising appears on everyone's Facebook page because the service is free for registered users. Advertisers take advantage of your profile information, or likes and dislikes, to effectively market their products or services to you. That's why your birthday is an important part of the required content. You do not have to click on any ads at any time, and can certainly spend all of your days on Facebook maneuvering around them.

However, if you would like to create an ad to be displayed on Facebook, it is a great way to reach your target audience that exists within the 900 million+ subscribers. Simply locate the previously mentioned "Advertise" link under the down arrow or "gear" icon and begin creating your ad. You will be asked specific questions about your product or service to insure its content is delivered to the right users. Pricing varies depending on the ad's reach, so take the time to familiarize yourself with the process. You can create an ad without activating it, if you would like to research the process before launching the campaign. There are plenty of great ebooks and helpful resources on the internet to assist in the process of creating a great Facebook ad.

Facebook Profile Changes 2013

The internet is constantly changing, and many websites do so to keep up with the times. In early-mid 2013, Facebook unveiled new changes to Facebook profiles in terms of the layout and other aspects. Keep in mind that this guide has general guidelines for how to use the social networking site, but that the Facebook website is constantly evolving and changing.

The main changes came for the timeline and overall layout, a design that was meant to help Facebook translate visually better to mobile devices, in addition to your laptop or computer.

So for example, you'll likely see a new left sidebar on your profile/timeline area, which has a listing of various icon images that you can click on to access various parts of your Facebook experience. Many of these components were touched upon throughout this guide, but here's a recap of what's on the sidebar area.

Lefthand Sidebar Components

At the very top of the left sidebar you'll see your user photo. Clicking on that will bring you to your Facebook profile.

To the right of your small photo profile is a "Lock" which will help you quickly access security and privacy settings for your account.

Next up, you'll see small images below. These include:

- News feed image - leads to your News Feed where you can see all the latest updates from friends and family.

- Messages image - Click this and it brings you to all of your messages.

- A calendar image that displays upcoming events that friends, family, or other connections/pages may have shared for you to attend.

- Images for any games or apps you may have associated with your Facebook account. Examples may be things like the Candy Crush game, or Words With Friends, or a Twitter app.

- You'll also see any Groups you are an administrator for, or member of possibly displayed in this left hand sidebar of icon images.

- Towards the very end of the sidebar you'll see "More" for more options including a way to see the latest status updates from various subsections of your Facebook friends, family and associates, as well as other people or pages you follow.

- The very last thing you may see at the bottom of the left sidebar will relate to chatting. You may see the option to "Turn on Chat" so you are available for live text chats with other people on your Facebook friends list. You'll then get a small search bar to search for any of your friends on chat, and you'll see a small square of icons showing you which friends are currently available for chat there.

- (To turn off chat, simply go to the lower righthand corner where you see "Chat" bar. Click on that bar, and it will expand your available friends chat list. On that bar, click the small "gear" at the top right and click on "Turn off chat." This will bring up a pop-up box menu allowing you to "Turn off chat for all friends" making you currently unavailable for online chats. There are also options there to turn off chat for certain parts of your Facebook friends list.)

By the way, don't worry if you aren't seeing a lot of things on your list, it may just mean you don't have any games or apps installed, or that you aren't running fan pages or special groups on Facebook.

Using Facebook on Mobile Devices

Facebook is currently available for a large number of mobile devices, including iPhones, iPads, iPad Mini, the Kindle Fire HD, various Android smartphones and other tablet devices. With that in mind, it's important to realize that having Facebook on a mobile device may be slightly different than having it for your desktop or laptop computer.

Many of the mobile devices mentioned may have Facebook integration built right in, so that you can simply enter your email and password from Facebook to have your mobile device connected with your Facebook at all times. In other instances, you'll need to obtain an app from the iTunes App store, or Google Play, Amazon, or other app store which is appropriate to your device.

What is the use of having a social networking account like Facebook if you cannot take it with you and show off your happenings to the word? Luckily, you can install Facebook on your iPhone, iPad or Android devices effortlessly, and use them interchangeably, without missing a beat.

How to Install/Sync Facebook on iPhone or iPad (newer models)

First things first, you are going to have to install the Facebook app to your Apple device, which can happen quickly. Simply tap on your "App Store" icon, and enter "Facebook" in the search store toolbar. Depending on which device you are using, be sure it is highlighted at the top of the page (iPad Apps or iPhone Apps). The store will usually default to your device, but it is worth it to double check.

Next, tap on the word "Free" to reveal the words "Install App" and tap the green button with that reference. Once the app downloads completely, tap on the Facebook App's icon to begin. You will have to enter your Facebook information to verify your account first, but as soon as you do, you will be ready to go!

All of the images, updates and newsfeeds will appear just as they do on your computer. However, in order to sync your contacts, birthdays and events to your iPhone or iPad from Facebook (which allows Facebook profile images to appear in the contacts area of your phone, adds birthdays and events automatically to your calendar) you must follow a few steps first.

On your device -- no matter which one you are using:

- Tap the Settings Icon.
- Scroll the Down the Left-hand Side's Toolbar to "Facebook."
- Tap Facebook.
- Move the Slider to "On" for Calendar, Contacts and Facebook.

You can also choose any apps you might want synced so when you play them on your computer, you start and finish in the same place as you would on your iPad or iPhone. Each of the items slid to the on position will automatically sync from Facebook to your iPhone or iPad or both as they update or change. You will not have to sync them on your own.

How to Install/Get Facebook for Android Phone

Android phones or tablets are very similar to the Apple versions, if only the programming and terminology are different. They both use Apps, and are both Facebook compatible. When you are ready to add Facebook to your Android phone or tablet, simply follow these couple of steps.

Locate the Google Play icon on your device, and tap it. Search the store for the Facebook App until it appears. Once it arrives, tap "Install" and wait for it to complete. You will have to verify your account by entering your Facebook username and password as well.

All of your information, photos, and newsfeed will remain the same as it is on your computer's Facebook account, and you will be able to post updates, images and videos directly from your phone or device effortlessly. Your Facebook account, including calendars, contacts and events will sync automatically as well, as long as you have your settings configured accordingly. To do so:

- Tap the Facebook App.
- Tap the Settings Icon.

- Check or Uncheck the Syncing you Desire for Calendar, Contacts and Apps.

You will not have to do this manually going forward, unless you want to change your settings at some point.

How to Install/Use Facebook on Kindle Fire HD

If your device of choice is the Kindle Fire HD, you can also enjoy the Facebook app on your tablet by downloading the app itself and signing in. First you will have to locate the Amazon Appstore on your device, and tap it to open. Once it is opened, search for Facebook. When it is revealed, tap "Get App" and allow it to download completely.

Once it has, enter your Facebook username and password to confirm your account, and begin using Facebook just as you would on your laptop or desktop computer. You can tap the app any time, and update your status as you see fit throughout the day, or whenever it occurs to you to check on the happenings around you.

How Does Graph Search Work?

New to Facebook users in July, 2013 is Graph Search. At the top of each Facebook page awaits an ever present search toolbar, which is indicated as such by the addition of the magnifying glass in the corner. Instead of a basic search previously performed on the site, which would allow you to look for people, places or things through a list of returned links, Graph Search is more intuitive and personalized for your specific profile.

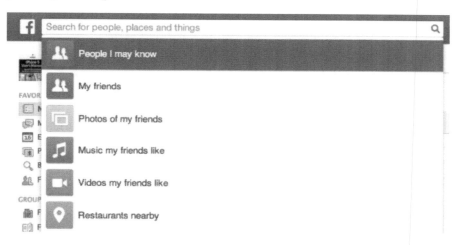

Graph Search allows you to search for people, places or things by searches using natural language. This means if you are looking for friends who like "insert brand name here" you will receive results that reflect that particular search. The results are a culmination of Facebook's one billion person user group, but more importantly your friends, likes, interests and profile information, and external search engine data that provides user specific results.

This means your searches reflect your online behavior, and help return results that you will be interested in, so you do not have to wade through the balance. This is more personalized than a Google, Yahoo! or Bing search that will return everything with the keywords you entered. This search is specific to your habits, and those of your Facebook friends first to give you the most definitive results available. Where it may fall short, the external search engine picks up the slack.

This search technique allows you to search places by name or location, check-ins from the user, the user's friends or places where either group has been tagged. It also provides objects with location information attached -- including those created or enjoyed by friends. It also gives access to the entire web directly, so you can literally search for anything or anyone.

You can use the search intelligence to be as specific as possible, say, "photos of my friends taken at beaches" or "Friends who like "How I Met Your Mother" or for something as generic as "CVS Drug Stores". It is completely up to you, and since Facebook serves as one of the largest search engines available, you are certain to receive the results you are looking for in some capacity.

The Reality of Facebook

Facebook is a fun way to keep in touch with everyone you know, and get to know people you have just met a little better. You can share pictures and videos, check in at restaurants and concerts, and even pop in from time to time to drop a few lines about what is going on around you.

The important thing to remember, however, is that everyone else has the exact same luxury, and you cannot control what they add to their profiles, or what they say in their status updates. You simply have to endure the rhetoric, opinions, ideas and concepts of everyone you have on your friends list, and all of the things they share.

If it all becomes too much, you can edit what you see in your timeline, and keep what you see tidy and clean, as a way of censoring the content you view. You can also "unfriend" individuals, or block them completely from seeing anything you write, or anything they write.

Lastly, if you really enjoy Facebook for all of the positives it provides, use your settings accordingly and only choose a select amount of people to be "friends" with you. For some, the object is to accumulate as many friends as possible, with zero regard for these half-strangers seeing your every thought, photo and connection. One way is not better than the other and each of the events, happenings or decisions you make on Facebook are completely up to you. Enjoy!

You're Ready to Navigate the Social Network!

Facebook is a fun and exciting way to stay in touch with friends, family and colleagues, while giving yourself the freedom to explore old relationships with classmates, or to seek new relationships with those with similar interests. The sky is the limit with a Facebook account, and since you are in control of the content you post, who you are friends with, and which people can see what you are doing, you should always feel safe and secure in your communications. It's a perfect opportunity to enjoy other people's updates, photos and happenings, while getting to send a few words of encouragement, congratulations or laughter, so what are you waiting for? Use this ebook to help sign up for an account today! You'll be glad you did, and so will all of the people who have missed you all of these years.

More Books by Shelby Johnson

iPhone 5 User's Manual: Tips and Tricks to Unleash the Power of Your Smartphone!

iPad Mini User's Guide: Simple Tips and Tricks to Unleash the Power of your Tablet!

Kindle Fire HD User's Guide Book: Unleash the Power of Your Tablet!

Kindle Paperwhite User's Manual: Guide to Enjoying your E-reader!

How to Get Rid of Cable TV & Save Money: Watch Digital TV & Live Stream Online Media

Chromecast Dongle User Manual: Guide to Stream to Your TV (w/Extra Tips & Tricks!)

Samsung Galaxy S4 User Manual: Tips & Tricks Guide for Your Phone!

Note: *All screen capture images in this ebook used as examples were obtained from the Facebook.com website.*

4879627R00044

Printed in Great Britain
by Amazon.co.uk, Ltd.,
Marston Gate.